Imagine a Butterfly

Stanford Apseloff

OHIO DISTINCTIVE PUBLISHING

Columbus, Ohio

For my son, Evan, and his beautiful mother, Sveta.

Text and photographs by Stanford Apseloff. In addition to butterflies in their natural habitats in Costa Rica, Mexico, and Ohio, this book contains photographs of butterflies taken at the Franklin Park Conservatory Blooms & Butterflies Exhibit in Columbus, Ohio.

No butterflies were touched or disturbed for any of the photographs.

To inquire about special discounts for bulk purchases, please contact Ohio Distinctive Publishing by email: special@ohio-distinctive.com or by phone: 614-459-3100.

10 9 8 7 6 5 4 3 2 1
032012-1-5000-JO-37040

Printed in the United States of America.

ISBN 978-1-936772-03-2

Library of Congress Control Number: 2012901873

Ohio Distinctive Publishing · 6500 Fiesta Drive · Columbus OH 43235
www.ohio-distinctive.com

Imagine you're young as the year you were born,
Now visiting a garden—the sun is warm.

Your hands are as small as butterfly wings,
And your eyes see clearly the tiniest things.

Imagine your garden grows all kinds of blooms
With pleasant scents of sweet perfumes.

And butterflies come from most everywhere—
All sizes and shapes, both common and rare.

A Monarch flies close; you watch it land—
Wings with white pearls, pumpkin and sand.

Then a Blue Morpho catches your eye,
Perched on a flower, wings raised high.

Brown with gold rings, but what's that inside?
You'll never imagine what these wings hide—

Clear blue sea and a black lava beach,
This Blue Morpho lands just out of reach.

Then two Morphos look like one—
A rendezvous in the midday sun.

Imagine more butterflies—dozens of types.
Picture their colorful patterns and stripes.

Imagine what each of them touches and sees,
The way they feel raindrops and summer's warm breeze.

Imagine seeing with butterfly eyes—
Thousands of lenses, the tiniest size.

They see without blinking, day after day,
Forward and backward and every which way.

Imagine you're drinking, as butterflies do,
The nectar of flowers or cool morning dew.

And then when you're done, there might be a trace
Of pleasant leftovers left on your face!

Sipping from flowers—that's common enough.
Orange Tigers taste some unusual stuff.

They drink from bird droppings, and in some cases,
They drink from the nostrils on animals' faces!

Two butterfly facts not everyone knows—
They taste with their feet and haven't got toes.

Everyone's heard of a tongue on a shoe,
But taste buds on feet—that's something new.

Imagine raindrops as big as your head.
Watch out for hail—seek sunshine instead.

Imagine a tailwind—what a relief.
You're surfing on air, light as a leaf.

Imagine a Monarch's journey in flight,
Thousands of miles, resting at night.

Relative to size, a hot-air balloon
Would be making a journey up to the moon.

Pretend your garden is under a spell,
Where jungle animals used to dwell,

Where birds and deer and cats with stripes
Are suddenly various butterfly types.

I see a tiger that magical power
Turned into a butterfly perched on a flower.

Then abracadabra!—what should appear?
A Peacock Butterfly, oh so near.

And this Queen, I imagine, once was a fawn,
A baby deer nibbling just after dawn.

Picture a hummingbird that's really a moth,
One that likes flowers more than wool cloth.

This Hummingbird Moth has its namesake's flair,
But is small like a bumblebee, and covered with hair.

Think what it's like to have meals in a bed
Of pretty pink mums, soft as silk thread,

Fluffy as feathers, scented for guests,
A perfect bed for butterfly rests.

This Buckeye Butterfly rests in a bed
Of pompom yellow and holiday red.

A lone dark cloud passes our way,
And the brown Buckeye body turns charcoal gray.

Brief darkness descends, and what do we see?
An Owl Butterfly perched in a tree.

Imagine your wings are works of art.
Perhaps they are formed in the shape of a heart.

Or maybe they look like fine stained glass,
Sprinkled with pollen the color of brass.

Perhaps you have that Swallowtail trait—
Two lower-wing tails, curved or straight.

Imagine your wings are a Glasswing's pair,
Like fragile ice, but even more fair.

This Glasswing Butterfly has nothing to hide;
Look through its wings to the other side.

Imagine clear wings with incredible speed—
A Hummingbird Moth that can hover and feed!

Maybe you're hanging in a forest's green shade
From the stem of a bloom or a leaf's lucky blade.

Imagine you're a butterfly as big as a sparrow,
Except for a body somewhat more narrow.

You're one of the Birdwing Butterflies
With bird-like flight and exceptional size.

And your black and green wings with their elegant taper
Are nearly as long as eleven-inch paper!

Now imagine your wings are black as the night,
With red at the bottom, both left and right.

Or maybe the black is brushed with blue
And daintily dabbed with yellow too.

Now pretend you're so small that few people notice.
Imagine some times that might be a bonus.

Your wings might seem small for a body so plump—
A bit too short to cover your rump.

Or maybe your wings reflect the sun's rays
To create an illusion of a fiery blaze.

Imagine your wings are slender and frail.
This one's a Postman but can't carry mail.

Pretend your wings are precious metals—
A fitting crown for flower petals.

Imagine your front legs and head are concealed
Almost as well as a mouse in the field.

Or maybe you look like a leaf that can fly.
Hiding is easy—you don't have to try.

Ghost Sulphur Butterflies blend with the scenery.
To casual observers, they're part of the greenery.

Imagine each bloom in a flowering bed
Is a hundred times bigger than your butterfly head.

Picture a perfect wedding outside.
Here comes a butterfly, fair as a bride.

Translucent gown and grand bouquet—
Will she stay or fly away?

Imagine now your favorite location—
A room, a house, a place to vacation.

And think how grander it would be
If filled with butterflies flying free.

Imagine the butterflies dancing on air
To the tune of the wind—graceful and fair.

Picture the wonder in a child's eyes
Who first sees flying butterflies.

Imagine that child once was you,
Next is your child, then grandchildren too.

Then go to a garden on a hot sunny day,
And you might see a butterfly pass by your way.

Or meander in meadows where wildflowers dwell
Because butterflies like that wildflower smell.

But if for some reason you simply can't go
To a garden or meadow that butterflies know,

Then this you can do instead anywhere—

Imagine a butterfly. Imagine you're there.